Above the Fold

by

Scott Ruescher

Finishing Line Press
Georgetown, Kentucky

Above the Fold

Copyright © 2025 by Scott Ruescher
ISBN 979-8-88838-904-1 First Edition
All rights reserved under International and Pan-American Copyright Conventions. No part of this book may be reproduced in any manner whatsoever without written permission from the publisher, except in the case of brief quotations embodied in critical articles and reviews.

Publisher: Leah Huete de Maines
Editor: Christen Kincaid
Cover Art: Charles Casey Martin
Author Photo: Judith McKernan
Cover Design: Elizabeth Maines McCleavy

Order online: www.finishinglinepress.com
also available on amazon.com

Author inquiries and mail orders:
Finishing Line Press
PO Box 1626
Georgetown, Kentucky 40324
USA

Contents

The 47 Bus 1

1:
My Eight-Year-Old Grandmother 5
Talisman 6
To the Editor of the *Plain City Advocate* 7
In the Stately Greek Revival Architectural Style 9
One Autumn Day Last year 11
At the Perryville Battlefield State Historic Site 13

2:
The Call 17
White Wooden Crosses 18
Above the Fold 19
Queen for a Day 20
The Orchard 22
Love Scenes 24
Tenskwatawa 26

3:
Traffic Jam 31
Game Called Because of Rain 32
At Hamilton and Pearl 33
First Impression 35
Earth Day 37
Screech Owl 39
The Trees of Heaven 41

4:
Plumbing 45
Injunction 46
At the Childhood Home of Ozzy Osbourne 48
The Sonnet 50
In the Southern-Most Mexican State of Chiapas 53
Tag 57

5:
Barrio Boston 61
Athens County Breakdown 64
Poplar Hollow Inventory 68
Soundtrack 72
The Oxford County Blues 76
Elegy for Omayra Sánchez 79

"It is difficult / to get the news from poems / yet men die miserably every day / for lack / of what is found there."

—William Carlos Williams

"I wanted to enter areas given over to prose writers, I wanted to talk about things the way a journalist can talk about things, but in poetry, not prose."

—C.K. Williams (as told to the New York Times, 2000)

The 47 Bus

At dawn one day that March, when the 47 bus went
By the house, standing room only, rear door and windows
Open for ventilation, I touched the cold glass
Of our picture window in pity, in unconditional admiration
For the people on board, fresh from beds and baths
And breakfasts of toast and coffee, who were streaking past
To work all day in the laundry rooms, laboratories,
And early morning emergency wards of hospitals spilled
Like pills across the hills of our locked-down city.

I wondered what song the tall Black technician in whites
Was bouncing up and down to with his earphones on,
How the plot of the popular purple romance novel
That the white nurse in pink was reading would unravel,
Whether the scenes in the Asian orderly's memory included
The shrimp-boat sunrise of a Mekong village in Vietnam,
And how the swim across the border might have haunted
The Mam-speaking Guatemalan woman responsible
For cleaning the surfaces of an ICU in her N95.

If I couldn't quite feel, through the motion-mural window,
Each sensation of the hybrid world they inhabited,
Maybe I could summon the telekinetic power
To steady their hands for the sutures they'd prepare
For surgeons all morning, give them the strength they'd need
To wheel carts of medicines through the sanitized halls,
The mental focus required to figure the results
Of blood tests and biopsies they'd file in digital folders
On terminals along the wall, and the knowledge and dexterity
To intubate patients connected to the ventilators.

I looked across the street, when the 47 bus had passed
Into the next block, through my own remote reflection
At the neighbors' homely house, its drab brown drapes drawn
Against the bright day, but kept my fingertips on the glass,
Wishing that the traces of those ephemeral faces
Had not been washed away from the surface so fast—
That I had had the chance to commemorate them,
To paint broad brush strokes on the glass in their honor,

Rendering indelible relevance to the abundant life within,
The sacrificial driver wishing everyone good morning,
And the bright yellow trim on the bus's white fenders.

1

My Eight-Year-Old Grandmother

In the only photograph I have of my great-great-grandfather
On my father's maternal side, taken on a summer day
Against the clapboard background of the house on Maple Street
That my father was born in, in Plain City, Ohio,
In 1919, I see, by light of a lamp on the kitchen table
On this winter night, my eight-year-old grandmother
Standing beside him and to his right in a white cotton dress,
A braid draping her shoulder, holding with her left hand
The back of the wooden chair that they've lugged outside
From the kitchen for him, smiling at the camera
With more warmth and pleasure than any of us ever knew her
In person to express, proud of the grisly old war veteran
With the long beard, the dark wool pants, the gaunt
Expression, and the dark wool coat he wears in spite of summer,
With his long legs crossed at the knee, and his hands
Hinged in his lap at the knuckles, likely still suffering
From ailments he's endured since returning from the war, including
The chronic rheumatism that he apparently incurred
On the cold march away from the most important of several
Relatively minor Civil War battles waged in Kentucky,
And the injury to his groin, at that same Battle of Perryville,
On October 8, 1863, that one unintentionally funny
Sentence or another describes in handwritten testimony
To suggest that a splinter of hickory from a split rail fence
Found its true destiny there when a rail was shattered
By a Confederate cannonball fired in his direction—ailments
I know about from reading the photocopied disability reports
That fell all around me like autumn leaves from a broadleaf tree
With photographs like the one I'm holding up to the light
When my history-buff mother died and left them all to me.

Talisman

At the end of my drive along the Blues Trail south
Through the cotton fields and shanty towns of the Mississippi Delta
From the nexus of Memphis in the southwest corner of Tennessee
Through Clarksdale, Indianola, and Cleveland, Mississippi,
By way of actual settings, around the college town of Oxford,
From Faulkner's fictional Yoknapatawpha County,
Where Byron Bunch, Lena Grove, Joe Christmas, Lucas Burch,
Joanne Burden, and Reverend Hightower played out
The complicated history of Jim Crow in the Deep South
In the novel *Light in August,* I gladly paid my entrance fee
To the Old County Courthouse Museum in Vicksburg
And, after bantering with the docent with a scripted jocularity,
Made my gradual way up the carpeted nearby staircase
Without the celerity stereotypical of a tourist from the North
One creaky riser at a time, to look at precious relics, in the first
Of four galleries, that were recovered from the gangrenous bodies
Of soldiers who died on the field or in hospital tents at the rear,
As if they were talismans that I could draw inspiration from—

As if artifacts from the corpses of conscripts recruited
From small-town cottage orchards, mosquito-crazed lumber camps,
Creek-side chicken farms, and paddle-splashed fishing docks
In Alabama and Pennsylvania, the Carolinas and Maine,
Vermont, Indiana, Michigan, the Dakotas, and Louisiana
Could do more than enthrall me with their anachronistic charm,
As if the buttons, hairbrushes, and combs, the boxes
Of hard tack, the tambourines, recorders, and corncob pipes,
The breast-pocket Bibles, dented canteens, and long dark strings
Of beef jerky still edible after one hundred and fifty years
Could take on an amusing but mystical significance
And blast me into orbit with understanding and clarity
When I moved from that cluttered gallery to the neater one
Across the hall, where black and white daguerreotypes
Of those martyred men, those foddered dead, awaited me on a wall.

To the Editor of the *Plain City Advocate*

Thanks to Warren Yoder, a Mennonite organic livestock farmer
Whose pacifist ancestors probably objected to the Civil War,
For pausing his work in the garden at the library for a minute
To answer my question about the approximate locations
Of the graveyards where the veterans in my ancestry are buried
And the street where my father was born at the end of World War I—
And for continuing from there with a tangential 20-minute discussion
Of sustainable agriculture—when I arbitrarily identified him
As the first lucky victim of my quest for connection here
And ambled over from the sidewalk with a nod of my head.

Thanks to the docent in the local historic society's storefront office
Between the Bible bookstore and the redneck bar on Main Street
For agreeing with me wholeheartedly, winking behind
Her husband's back, that the McMansion subdivisions
Filling up the fields on the edge of town, along Big Darby Creek
Where my first-generation German American grandfather
Hunted turtles for soup when courting my local grandmother,
Were at least as ugly as sin when I dropped by to see
If anyone knew where the beer-drenched pool hall used to be
That one of my grandmother's more adventurous older sisters,
With two of her younger, rather dissolute brothers, ran.

Thanks to the chubby farmer on the seat of his John Deere tractor,
At rest with his helper and son in his Adams Road barnyard
After a morning of haying or bringing in the soybeans,
For calling on his cell phone his equally elderly neighbor, Marge,
To see if she might know where the 200-acre farm
And the red-brick farmhouse with white wooden trim might be
That, according to family papers bequeathed unto me
Many years before, belonged to my great-great-grandfather
On my father's mother's side, when I pulled up and hopped out,
With a little more enthusiasm than I probably should have,
Of the rusted white hybrid 2007 Toyota Prius
That my wife and I won in a Boston public-radio raffle on WBUR—
And thanks to him for saying, with reference to the license plates,
When I came back from checking out the cabin across the creek
That his ancestors acquired from the original homesteaders
After they moved to the area in the early 1850s,
"Massachusetts, huh? Isn't that where Biden's from?"

And thanks to everyone else in Plain City, Ohio, the seat
Of Union County, thirty miles northwest of the capital, Columbus,
Where those ancestors on my father's side who fought for the Union
In the Civil War are buried—not just that great-great-grandfather
But his father as well, and two of my great-great-uncles
Who died, according to my records, in unnamed battles
Somewhere in the South—and where I wish I'd been
When the whole town showed up for the coming-home parade
In late April of 1865, now that the lilacs in the dooryards
Had just begun to bloom, and the forsythia to fade.

In the Stately Greek Revival Architectural Style

Up steep Clay Street, perpendicular to the main drag
On the south side of downtown, I was jogging in the general
Direction of the battleground at the Vicksburg National
Military Park, site of the Union's decisive blockade
Of supplies that would have kept the Confederates in power
On the Mississippi River, when I found myself passing
Two solid blocks of grand and comfortable mansions built
In the stately Greek Revival architectural style.

Eager as always for connections to the present, I recalled
That this particular style, characterized by a wide porch
And four white columns, from the 1820s to the 1850s,
Was popular among the rulers of the antebellum South
If also responsible for the building we inhabit
On a corner back in Cambridge, one of the capitals
Of the abolitionist cause, that the prominent Harvard poet
And professor of literature and Romance languages,
Henry Wadsworth Longfellow, might have visited
When traveling from Brattle Street in his horse-drawn carriage
To see Washington Allston work on his paintings.

That might have been, I surmised while crossing the street
Into a wooded block, around the time when Allston,
An 1800 Harvard grad from a Carolina rice plantation,
Looking for the inspiration he'd found as an undergrad,
Was living out the final thirteen years of his life
In a studio catty-corner from us, now the site
Of a row of brick townhouses known as Allston Terrace—
About a century or so, I thought as I glanced
At four more white columns on another broad porch,
Before our house, built as a duplex, was turned into a triplex
To accommodate the office of a neighborhood physician,
Known as Dr. Fredd, that makes up all but two rooms
Of our first-floor abode at Magazine and William.

This, I remembered, since one thing leads to another
In associations as in streets, was after Allston made it big
For twenty years in England, partly for that portrait
Of Samuel Taylor Coleridge that you see on the cover

Of the first of two volumes of Holmes's definitive
Biography of him, but also for the grand romantic paintings
Of Biblical and mythical subjects, among the first collected
By Brahmins for the MFA and the Boston Athenaeum.

Now it occurred to me, entering the ornate gate
Of the national park, that Allston's allegorical paintings
Would have been more than suitable for framing
On the walls of the mansions on either side of Clay Street
That were spared from shelling, according to the travel guide,
By Union gunboats in the river below the bluff,
When Grant learned that the wealthiest civilians, albeit
Those who profited most from the slavery system,
Were hiding underneath them with their precious belongings.

Inside the park, I ran on the road for self-guided auto-tours
From one monument to soldiers from specific states
To another, among rows of upright white rectangular tablets,
Imagining the aristocrats sighing with relief
In their furnished bunkers when they heard the news
That Grant had pardoned them from additional shelling,
Even though—or maybe because—they were keeping,
In those tunnels under Vicksburg, along with jewels, linens,
And substandard imitations of Allston paintings,
The servants, the slaves, the shackled human beings
Who might have been cousins of the Black descendants,
For all they knew, who worked near the coast, a few hundred
Miles east of Vicksburg, on the Allston plantation
That—or so I've gathered from research since my return—
Is currently being subdivided for luxury condominiums.

One Autumn Day Last Year

I think I cherish most, as the archaic language of letters
Displayed in glass cases at battleground museums
In the American South would have it, and to my breast
Hold dearest—as a soldier might have written his mother or lover
To reassure her that he was reading the Bible or looking
At her picture—the moment at the Harvard Art Museum, here
In Cambridge, Massachusetts, one autumn day last year,
When Arielle Jiang, a classical musician and arts education
Student from China, whose first name in Mandarin, Xueer,
Is supposed to be pronounced more or less as "Schweer,"
Studying, in a gallery of prints and paintings by Winslow Homer,
Snippets of sheet music from some of those songs
That he illustrated for an issue of *Harper's Weekly*
During the Civil War, at my request put her soft porcelain face
As close as she was allowed to the frame on the wall
To inspect the measures between the graphic vignettes
Which Homer had drawn with maudlin grace in the margins
And to proceed to sight-read effortlessly, in a melodious whisper
That was sure not to attract the attention of the guards,
Not the melody to *The men will cheer, the boys will shout,*
The ladies they will all turn out, with that lyric about
All of us feeling gay again, in the original meaning of a word
I would have been happy to define for her, if she hadn't already
Known its connotation for "homosexual" or "queer,"
And not the rousing, exclamatory shout of that song,
"When Johnny Comes Marching Home Again, Hurrah, Hurrah!",
But, with a quiet gusto that a soldier might have given it
Had it been a special song from the patriotic repertoire
Of Genghis Khan's troops marching the Silk Road
In the thirteenth century, or of Mao Tse-tung's Red Army
Conquering Chiang Kai-shek less than a century before,
The refrain of another song, "Battle Hymn of the Republic,"
That I first learned to sing back in elementary school,
In Westerville, Ohio, in 1962 or so, with those rousing lyrics
By Julia Ward Howe that were known to be a favorite
Of Abraham Lincoln's (sung to the tune of "John Brown's Body"),
And had come to love even more since seeing it become
The source, in 1968, in that farewell speech he gave

To the Memphis sanitation workers the night before he died,
Of Martin Luther King's claim that his eyes had seen the glory
Of the coming of the Lord, as Xueer was claiming now.

At the Perryville Battlefield State Historic Site

When I asked him where the father of my father's mother's mother
Might have been fighting when he took one where it counts
For the Abolitionist cause, I couldn't have been happier
To see the long-haired librarian in his plaid shirt, sneakers,
And wrinkled khakis roll his considerable bulk,
In a three-wheeled swivel chair that served as a helpful
Extension of his body, first to the old desk-top computer
To look it up in his database and match the number
Of the Union troop that he was likely to have been in
(With other conscripted soldiers from the tiny rural farm town
Of Plain City, Ohio) with a battlefield map
That indicated which platoon was standing where—
And then, after that, and then, then and there, to see him roll
All the way from the computer, across the expanse
Of indoor-outdoor carpeting in the museum's basement library,
To a screen door that looked out on a pleasant summer day,
And to see him point up to a small gray goat barn in a corner
Of a pasture and say, without even turning to look at me
Or to appreciate the humorous beauty of the goats looking back, that
That's where the troop of conscripted farmers and carpenters,
Mechanics, handymen, coopers, clerks, teachers, and merchants
Who may never have seen a Black person in their lives,
Unless on a trip to Columbus or outside of a church stop
On the Underground Railroad, were standing when a cannonball
From a Confederate artillery post down toward the road
Hit the split-rail hickory fence that in turn projected a splinter
In the exact direction, according to the photocopies
Of his annual pension papers, of my great-great-grandfather's groin—
An anecdote that finally got him, hearing me relate it
At the screen door while his back was still turned, to turn around
And look at me with a most quizzical expression.

2

The Call

When I go back for a late autumn visit, and a cold breeze is blowing
The red and yellow leaves from the lawns on the south
To the fields on the north side of town, in my imported car
I want to go with it, on the Old 3C, five miles beyond
The small-town limit, all the way to the farmhouse at Africa and Plum
Along the Underground Railroad where, thirty years after
The runaways had gone, my grandfather was born—

To that quaint white clapboard affair with the limestone foundation,
The red barn in back, and the black Dodge at the side,
Up a gravel driveway in a grove of stately maples granted
Clemency for their shade, fringed by a pruned hedge
Of rose bushes and blackberry vines, on land holding its own
In the sprawl of Delaware County, north of Columbus,
Till developers decide how to divide it like the farms on every side;

To the pump at the well by the door at the side, to the outhouse
And the chicken coop entangled in stray grape vine,
Near the root cellar where, in sterilized jars, his mother stored pickles
And berries she'd jammed, and beyond it all, past the barnyard
Where hens and roosters, Rhode Island Reds, pecked at scattered corn,
To a break of box elders and an Osage orange hedge,
And to the higher field they planted in winter wheat in fall—

All of it waiting for me here in the car on the shoulder of the lane
Putting it in neutral to wait for the call, idling out front,
For five or ten minutes, in hopes that he might step, his school books
In hand, from the shut front door out across the stubbled yard,
To the wagon he hitched to the workhorse at dawn,
Already a capable young man, good with figures and languages,
Already thinking of moving with my grandmother to the city,

As if it were a chilly Tuesday October morning in 1911,
And he was going to let the mare find the way while he studied
His Latin; as if the furrows of the fallow fields on both sides
Have not been planted in new houses and are still vanishing
In one-point-perspective toward the horizon, draining in a glance
My glimpse of his past with a plough-perfect power
That could drain half my heritage straight down a groundhog's hole.

White Wooden Crosses

At one such shrine, at one such cluster of white wooden crosses,
At one such perilous hairpin turn in the steep Clinch Mountains,
I peered over the side of the cliff as my father steered to the right,
As my mother beside him in the passenger seat held on tight,
And as my sister behind him, to my left, lifted her bright
Eyes from her book, and imagined myself a medic pulling up
From the hospital in the valley, fifteen minutes after the accident,
In a white ambulance with the siren wailing, the red lights flashing.

Hopping out on the passenger's side when my buddy puts it
In park, I line the orange caution cones across the narrow road
To keep the oncoming traffic from nudging us over the edge,
Strap on my backpack of emergency medical supplies,
And unload the gurney from the back, tying it to the rappelling rope.

Then we go unraveling down the mountain through the scree,
Kicking loose rock and small stones free, pocking puffs of dust,
And pushing off from the wall with our well-treaded boots
On a slope too dramatic, an incline too deep, to support
The vegetation that would keep it from eroding, taking the same
45-degree route that the driver down the mountain took,
That the casualties always take, the tourists, teenagers, and truckers
Who lose control of vehicles and plunge through the guardrail,
Until we come to rest on a broad flat outcropping of rock
Beside the crumpled cab of a trucker, a man who approached
The hairpin turn in his 18-wheeler at an inaccurate angle—

A man said by the preacher, at his funeral on the main street
Of Bristol, Tennessee, or Bristol, Virginia, depending which side
Of the street his family prefers, to have been an honest Christian man,
A good dad, a deer hunter, a faithful loving husband to boot,
Moderate with moonshine, funny, and a baseball coach as well,
And such a fan of country that we reportedly found Patsy Cline
Serenading him with "Sweet Dreams" from Nashville,
On WSM, 650 on his radio dial, when we wedged open the door
On the driver's side of the cab with the jaws of life
To find him thrown across the console to the floor like a rag doll.

Above the Fold

Midway between the dates of the Kent State shootings
And my high school graduation, I was sitting down to eat lunch
At the Formica table in my mother's yellow kitchen—
Leftover Johnny Marzetti, that famous Italo-Midwestern
Macaroni concoction—from a green plastic bowl
On the last day of December, during Christmas vacation,
When I saw, in the frontpage headline spanning the width
Of the Columbus Dispatch, in bold and italicized caps,
More bad news from the Appalachian hollers three hours south—
38 MINERS KILLED IN KENTUCKY EXPLOSION.
There was a line below, in plain text, indicating the exact
Location of the mine—at Hurricane Creek, outside of Hyden,
In Leslie County, in the poorest district of Eastern Kentucky.
And, under that, the article suggesting that the blast,
According to inspectors, occurred when a stray electrical spark
From a piece of deep-mining machinery, a cutter, a scraper,
Or some other piece of equipment that the men in my family
Had been making for fifty years on sheet-metal lathes
At Jeffrey Manufacturing Company near downtown Columbus,
Ignited a cloud of coal dust gases, asphyxiating instantly,
If not incinerating, turning to ash, everyone in the shaft, including
The good-looking guys in the photograph beside that
Whose euphonious names I invoke in their memory.
I don't remember which four of the 38 appeared
In the photograph exactly—whether Alonzo Couch, Kermit
Hubbard, Teddy Bush, and Delbert Henson, embodiments
Of a rambunctious male culture more than permutations
Of some incestuous genealogy that some prefer to know them for;
Maybe Grover Bowling, Walter Hibbard, Rufus Jones, and Theo
Griffin, gathered for a Polaroid in front of the company store,
Backs to the gravel road that disappears in the right-hand corner;
Or Decker Whitehead, Arnold Sizemore, Lawrence Gray,
And Denver Young, leaning my way in clodhoppers
And blue denim jackets. Whichever four, they squint for the camera
In the red autumn sunshine still, big healthy boyish smiles
In their coal-blackened faces, mops of happy hair fringing
Their golden helmets, joined at the shoulder in symmetrical order
Like carbon molecules in a covalent bond that has to endure
Constant pressure for millions of mineral years before
It can even begin to think about turning into diamonds.

Queen for a Day

The first time I saw Tabloid Mary, I mean the first time
I really recognized her enormous potential
For iconic bronze statuary, an archetypal model
Of rural American poverty, one afternoon in 1962
As I sat on the couch watching television in a trance
And nibbling toward the center of a peanut butter sandwich
After my school day at Whittier Elementary was through,
I knew we were in trouble. I was only eight years old,
Not particularly precocious, never known to have been
Inclined toward a life as a medium for the divine.
And it would be another year before the assassination.
But I knew we were in trouble. If she could go on TV,
For God sakes, for everyone in the nation to see,
And make a complete and utter fool of herself, in a gown
Of royal purple satin and Cinderella's own glass heels,
With a crown of precious jewels on her precarious head,
Telling the drop-dead-handsome host of *Queen for a Day*
That for as long as she could remember, *since practically forever*,
She had been enchanted by Elvis's voice and face
And that he *sure as shootin'* was welcome to drop by her place
Whenever he happened to be passing through town,
Then we were really in for it. I mean, if she could have dressed
In the black polyester slacks that had only recently come
Into synthetic fashion, the dollar-store flip-flops,
And the floral pullover top that she usually wore
To hang around the house watching *General Hospital*,
As the World Turns, and *The Days of Our Lives*
With her mousy-brown mop of hair up in curlers all day,
Now that the holler had been given good TV reception,
Behaving as she did when home alone in her mountain hamlet
In eastern Kentucky, where no one could see her rise
From her second-hand couch with busted springs to sit
At the Formica table by her coal-burning stove
Drinking a cup of Nescafe and reading about Elvis
And his problems with his lovers in the *National Enquirer*—
I might have felt differently. But as things stood, I knew
That there really was no point in saving this nation.

Even if there was something charitable in the choice
To take patronizing pity on a poor rural woman,
To remove her from her natural habitat in the holler
A three-hour drive from the city, to fly her first class
To Los Angeles from Lexington and dress her up like that
In a two-thousand dollar Hollywood-designer dress,
To give her a luxury bedroom suite, a brand-new Cadillac,
An all-expenses-paid two-week Caribbean cruise,
And a Technicolor television window on the world—
Still, the whole thing was a mess. We really did lack
The "peasant traditions" that would have given us
Americans some character, as I would later learn the poet
William Carlos Williams in his poem "To Elsie" had had it.
We had surrendered ourselves to the adoration of celebrity
That I would later learn an artist named Andy Warhol
And his assistants at a studio called The Factory were mocking
In Greenwich Village, in New York City, in silkscreen prints
In various combinations of washed-out pastel colors.

Multiple Chairman Maos, for instance. Many Marilyn
Monroes, of course. A bunch of Nelson Rockefellers
And Jackie Kennedys, countless Campbell's soup cans
And enough Elvis Presleys to keep us in sarcastic stiches.
Double Elvis, Triple Elvis, 8 Elvises, and *Elvis Eleven Times*—
All variations on a black-and-white still of the star
Posing in the attitude of the spaghetti-western sheriff,
In boots, bandanna, jeans, chaps, and a cowboy shirt, planting
His feet wide apart and giving us that mischievous grin
That had already charmed the nation, drawing a pistol
From a holster in one of the ridiculous movies
He made in Hollywood in the 1960s and 70s,
After he'd made a killing on the rock-solid top-40 list
With "Don't Be Cruel," "I Got a Woman," "Heartbreak Hotel,"
And a dozen other covers of Black rhythm and blues tunes.

Not to mention *Red Elvis*, a nearly six-foot-tall silkscreen
Owned by a billionaire collector in Connecticut
That features a six-by-six grid of 36 black-and-white
Headshots of the King on a monochromatic background.

The Orchard

When I happen upon Elvis's ubiquitous image
 In unexpected places, if it's depicted in the midst
Of a lip-curling twist on stage or a full-throated shout
On a life-sized piñata in front of a bodega
In the capital of Guatemala, or if I happen to see it
Minding its own business on a scarecrow in a garden
On a back-country road in Maine in the White Mountains
Near the Chatham Valley border with the state of New Hampshire,
Or say I glimpse a chipped plaster bust of Elvis in his prime
Overlooking a canal from an Amsterdam window,
Or hear his voice escaping from the strangest places made
Familiar by his presence, from the screened-in porch
Of a trailer on a road that ends at the ocean shore
On the coast of Rhode Island, for instance, on the coast
Of Oregon, or on the coast of Galveston, Texas, Biloxi,
Mississippi, or the Delmarva or Olympic Peninsulas, even,
Or if I hear one of his unintentionally funny tunes come
From the rolled-down window of a hot-rod in a hick town
In Ohio, Idaho, Iowa, Utah, Nevada, or Indiana,
From the radio of a lifeguard at an outdoor swimming pool
In some gated McMansion community in Suburbia,
Or from the doorway of a vintage Cambridge record store
Known for stocking Motown, Muscle Shoals, and Stax recordings—

Then I remember my adolescence, when I was still able
To put away the Beatles, the Stones, the Kinks, and the Animals,
Lower a stack of vintage 45s down on the turntable,
And travel back in time, ten years before my own generation's,
All the way back to Elvis's prime, to find myself
 In a brand-new '57 Ford Fairlane Town Sedan,
Cherry red, forest green, or an almost iridescent bottle-fly blue,
With white-walled tires, bucket seats, and four on the floor
Driving out of town with Donna, Lucy, Anita, Deb,
Or Peggy Sue at my side, bubble gum popping
From her perpetual pout, an unsmoked cigarette
Tucked behind my ear, skipping school on a fall afternoon,
The sun gleaming on the hood and the wing-like fenders,
The landscape of farmland and new suburban tracts
Spooling off the windshield like reeled frames of a movie,

The windows all rolled up to keep in and amplify
The sound of his latest top-40 hit, "It's All Right," "Don't Be Cruel,"
Or "Blue Suede Shoes," playing on the radio,
A mud-stained sleeping bag in the back seat ready
To be spread out in an aisle of an orchard in the grass,
Where the two of us will be willing, eager, and able
To offer each other bites of an ordinary apple, a Cortland, Empire,
Or MacIntosh, yet to be pecked, busheled, and sold
At wholesale warehouse prices, with a pleasure that will keep us
From worrying too much, as some of our elders seem
To wish we'd have the sense to finally start doing,
About the direction this country seems to be going.

Love Scenes

Even though that corny song by the Everly Brothers
Was already an oldie, I sang its maudlin initial verse aloud to myself,
When I want you in my arms, / When I want you and all your charms,
With a visceral yearning that I have nursed ever since,
Starting home alone with my soft vanilla ice cream cone
After the crowd of loud kids at the Dairy Queen had dispersed.

As I passed the houses on Park Street where my pale math teacher
And a pretty girl who'd moved there from Tennessee lived,
I sang the awful second verse too, *When I feel blue in the night,*
And I need you to hold me tight, with my heart still burning
And my mouth making its way down the spiral of cold white cream—
And when I crossed the playground of Whittier Elementary School,
Turned onto East Walnut, and approached my block,
I made the most of my loneliness by singing the refrain,
Whenever I want you, Whenever I need you, All I have to do is dream,
Which almost kept my tears from falling from my eyes like salty rain.

Crossing the yard of our house under the spreading ash tree, I pictured
The red-hot love scenes that must have been rolling
In the cinematic back seats of automobiles on the edge of town
Long after the lovers had finished their ice cream sandwiches
And had fed each other the cherries on top of their shared banana splits—
Among the yellow school buses in the gravel lot behind
The big cement football stadium; in a lane of tall black walnut trees,
In the shadow of a barn that still had bales of hay in its lovesick loft
Long after the farmer moved into the nursing home
And sold all of his property off; and out at the Hoover Reservoir
That the bulldozers had made by damming Big Walnut Creek
A century after my ancestors planted its banks in grain
When they came by ox-drawn wagon from the Potomac in Virginia.

Without a mouth to kiss, without a lover to call my own,
Working my way down, with my lips and my tongue, to the sugar cone,
I repeated the refrain, stepping toward the stoop in a trance,
Whenever I want you, /Whenever I need you,/ All I have to do is dream,
Just as you could hear it sung any Friday at a high school dance.

Taking my first bite of the cone as I opened the door,
I walked on tiptoes through the living room and the kitchen
To the top of the basement stairs, picturing the girls of my dreams
Giggling and groping in the back seats of those cars with their boyfriends.

And I repeated the refrain again in my descent to the basement,
All I have to do is dream, stressing that part of the chorus,
Dream dream dream, three melodious times
Before repeating it again, a fourth extended time,
But this time with emphasis, this time with feeling,
Isolating the diphthong three distinct times, giving it its own
Symbolic, somatic, polysyllabic importance, *drea-ea-ea-ea-eam*,
As if to suggest a sense of drifting away at peace
From a lovesick reality too depressing to experience.

Dream dream dream, drea-ea-ea-ea-eam, I sang to myself
In my lonesome bed in the basement, slipping under
M shroud-like sheet, my cloud-like covers, imagining the radios
Of all three parked cars tuned to the same station, *WCOL, 1230
On your AM dial*, all three couples sitting up in the back seats,
While the fireflies flashed their green lights of approval,
At staggered intervals, in the windshield of each car,
To sing along with the tune the deejay had announced,
A golden moldy Top 40 oldie by the Everly Brothers
That everyone still loved, that everyone still sang along with.

Dream dream dream, drea-ea-ea-ea-eam, I sing to this day
When I hear the song on the radio, or when I see those photographs
Of Phil and Don Everly in their trim suits, pompadours,
And thin ties, with their great acoustics and harmonized vocals,
And with the immortal Chet Atkins on rhythm guitar..

Tenskwatawa

Having, at the time, absolutely no career ambition
To be a doctor, an architect, a teacher, a politician,
Or a law-practicing poet who forges sociological connections
Between logic and emotion, ordinarily I would have paid
Less attention to the history teacher's presentation of the chapter
On the manifest destination of the colonial platoon
Setting out from Boston, under the direction
Of Rufus Putnam, in their Conestoga, ox-drawn wagons
To follow the native foot trail from Fort Pitt
At the confluence of the Monongahela and the Allegheny
Along the beautiful river known by the Seneca as the Ohio,
Than I would have to the sight of Eddie, the charismatic custodian,
Passing in the hallway with his four-wheeled bucket
And his wig-like mop, my classmate Karen crossing
Her perfectly proportioned legs across the aisle from me,
And the spring warblers outside the classroom window
Picking caterpillars from the blossoms of the crabapple tree.

But when he told how they set up camp on the picturesque bank
Of the Ohio at Marietta, then infiltrated Indian land
In the Northwest Territories from that fort at the mouth
Of the tributary Muskingum, in the process paving the way
For the invasion of larger troops of colonial soldiers
Who eventually would encounter, before the turn
Of the 19th century, the warriors behind Tecumseh,
The chief of the Shawnee Indians, who attempted to lead
The indigenous nations, in confederacy with the British,
Against the colonists' incursions, but who failed to unite them
And got so disheartened by that and by the defeat
To William Henry Harrison at the Battle of Tippecanoe,
And by the broken treaty with Mad Anthony Wayne
That he led his diehard followers from the Greenville camp
North of present-day Dayton near the Indiana border
To the Battle of Fallen Timbers near present-day Toledo,
And even farther north to an Ontario still known
As Upper Canada then, to the Battle of the Thames,
In October of 1813, only to be ambushed by a white man, shot
In the heart with a rifle, and taken to a makeshift wigwam

Of poplar saplings and deer hides, to die in the arms
Of his brother Tenskwatawa, the Shawnee medicine man,
Also known as The Prophet, who accurately predicted
The two enormous earthquakes, in 1811 and 1812,
That radiated from their epicenter in New Madrid, Missouri,
On the western bank of the Mississippi River—

Then I put my distractions aside and finally started to listen.

3

Traffic Jam

From the hollow iron railing of a riveted green bridge
High above the river, I could see Mars, red and mad
In the clear black sky in the east above the harbor,
Attempting to appear—on Valentine's night, without my lover here—
Equidistant to the pregnant white full moon in the sky
(To whom he was about as near as he's ever allowed in a year)
And the blinking red light on the roof of the university library
That warns planes and cherubs not to enter the atmosphere.

And I could see cars, on both banks of the black river,
With moonlike headlights and Mars-like taillights headed to and fro
The candlelit city, the celestial occupants fresh from thawing out
The ice-white sheets of their beds, dressed, I guessed,
In the red skirts and trousers, the white shirts and pullovers,
That are known to yoke the astral, complementary powers—
Earthbound wooers who'd snared their share of starlight from the sky
Now intent on romantic public restaurant dinners.

Below me I saw a snow-white flock of hand-fed geese
For whom the cold had not quite sealed the river shut just yet
Floating upon a still black pool near the lace collar of white ice
Around a gray granite pylon—and through a window a scholar,
Oblivious, I imagined, to everything but the love story
He was reading in a book, looking, in a library nook, with lonely eyes
On the comings and goings of woman and man, too hurt, too prone
To lamentation, and too shy to participate in the ultimate traffic jam.

Game Called Because of Rain

It was pouring like crazy, that summer day in Kenmore Square,
On the slender vendor with greased-back hair, when I walked through
On the way back to Cambridge. A decade before the curse
Of the Bambino on the Red Sox was finally broken, it was raining
As it had hardly ever rained before, soaking him to the skin,
Saturating his sidewalk stand of card tables and plastic crates,
And deterring fans from fighting over the ponchos and umbrellas
That he'd added to his lair of wishful pennants, Louisville bats,
Bright red socks, and red, white, and blue Tuscan-typeface baseball hats.

Across the glistening hoods of their square sedans I saw
The Greek American seafood place with the plaster bust of Plato
In the plexiglass window, with the plaster model of the Parthenon;
Next to that, the vacant parking lot that the rain was in the process
Of transforming to an oily pond. Two doors down, the student bookstore,
Mannequins staffing its window display, and then the dingy bar
Where a vendor could nurse, in off-season benders, a stiff drink
That lasts about as long as an inning of scoreless boredom
That sluggers smash to pieces with swings that make the stadium boom.

Like him I knew that the team was doomed, the rain seeming to fall
Just to keep the season going down the drain—that no eager kid,
Stuck in the traffic jam, would dash from a car with his dad's cold cash
In a downpour like this, unless for a souvenir promised with great
    insistence.

He was still hawking when I walked through, throwing his call
All the way across the cars, like a ground ball thrown by a third baseman
Across the head of the pitcher to get the runner in time at first,
Or by an outfielder who catches the fly at the wall and nails,
With a single bounce to the catcher, the runner who tagged up at third
And tried to run home. But when his calls vanished in the traffic,
Like foul balls that disappeared in the sprawling thorns behind the field
Where he played as a kid, I wondered if the vendor would crawl
On hands and knees between the cars to chase them all down
Like he did as a boy with a bat, tires revolving by his head so close
He could see the resemblance that the poets all speak of.

Gravel stuck in tire tread. Unsung syllables caught in our throats.

At Hamilton and Pearl

Outdoors in shorts and tank top all summer, Henry hoed the rows
Of his plum tomato garden. He loosened the soil at the base
Of each plant. He watered around the roots before the sun had a chance
To swing around south. He served the plants manure tea
And mulched them with fertilizer from his compost heap.

We saw him from the kitchen window during breakfast on weekends,
Elbows and knees bent to the task, a warm white octogenarian
Sun-ripened Italian man, retired since the Seventies or so,
Who gardened, he said, "because it keeps me on my toes."

He had ears like snail shells and a nose like a hyacinth bulb,
Legs like knobby carrots, arms like parsnips, and a pension from a firm
That he tallied credits and debits for—and lived, we supposed,
On the meals his sister, Margaret, prepared for him upstairs,
In the second-floor apartment of the two-story yellow house
At Hamilton and Pearl. He liked chicken, salad, and pasta sauced
With his own plum tomatoes and homegrown garlic and basil.

Sometimes we saw him handing over bouquets of cultivated flowers
To the girls, old and young, who passed in seed and blossom
On the sidewalk of our thoroughfare—peonies and dahlias, acacias
And mums—with shy smiles, extended arms, and friendly phrases
Of everyday wisdom, formalities as familiar as the sunlight of summer.

It was none of our business, really, what Henry had been doing
For love for all those years. Was he a confirmed straight bachelor
Who couldn't be bothered, or a *magna cum laude* alumnus
Of the old school of queers? All we knew for certain was
That he marked the seasons with the blooming of his flowers,
From daffodil, crocus, and tulip, to lily, iris, and peony.

He was decisive in speech and action, self-reliant and independent,
And seemed to value intuition and reason in equal measure,
Buzzing around the garden like a bee all morning
With his watering can in hand, and his spade and claw in a bucket

Sooner or later his roses bloomed too, and then Henry handed them,
All the way opened, to the beautiful neighbor women

He sometimes even knew by name. Those that remained,
When his girls had gone in for supper, he scattered along the prim hedge
Of the privet hedge he'd groomed with his pair of sharpened sheers,
If not with a pair of scissors, along the sidewalk in front.

By November, when the hedge's prickly foliage at the edges
Curled and fell, we saw the bare aluminum wires of the fence
For what they were—cautions not to invade the privacy
Of a man who'd rather deadhead petunias and talk about the weather.

First Impression

To court her the way she liked, I didn't have to rearrange
The whole New England landscape behind her in the distance
To make her prettier or more elemental than she already was.
With help from dramatic angles and juxtapositions of radiant lines,
I wasn't forced to give her nose less emphasis, her affinity
With nature more, or her diminutive stature the grand illusion
Of a statue's proportions. She didn't make me see, in the background
Of our beginnings, beyond a choppy bay, a stark coniferous regiment
Of fir trees marching to meet the salted assault of the surf.
She never once insisted that a placid lake be behind her
Whenever I spoke to her, bowing graciously like a quack romantic,
Careful not to crack with a climactic sweep of my arm
The fragile breeze in the summer air. No requisite birch canoe or two.
No absolutely essential loons. No mandatory matrimonial moons.

Except for grape and honeysuckle climbing the fence below,
Little but Norway maple and celandine and ragweed grew
In the triple-decker neighborhood outside her third-floor windows
Where I got my first impression. Even ailanthus trees
Had a hard time growing, in cinders cast from old coal furnaces.
But from her kitchen sink, when I stood to get a drink, I could see
The flowering black locust trees planted along the curb
At intervals in the sidewalk bricks, some linden trees languishing
By the basketball court, and in the distance a few blocks away
The bushy slew of indigo on the bank of the regurgitated river,
Where bums from broken mill towns camped in cardboard tents.
At night if you were lucky, she said you could make out
Venus on the horizon, and two or three of the brighter stars.
I was not about to doubt her. For I had been about a mile from nature
When she brought me down to earth with gravity at her table
By a windowless wall with particle-board wainscoting
And a red rural Brueghel print above it like a mural.

In her Cambridge kitchen, at a table set with baba ganoush,
Guacamole, sourdough bread, Kalamata olives, and bowls
Of minestrone soup, when she described her rural childhood
On a ridge-top piece of land in southern New Hampshire,
She didn't ask me to see, in her green eyes, pools of cold brook water
With speckled eggs of granite on the sands at the bottom.

She didn't ask me to compare the movement of her hands, fluttering
When she spoke, to swallows or butterflies, or their color to that
Of beech leaves still attached to their twigs in the middle of winter.
She didn't say she got her grin from some toothy beaver
Or her tufted auburn hair from the wind-combed hummocks
I'd seen in the snow on a frozen swamp on my skis in the winter
When everything in sight but the beech leaves, the blue sky,
And the drooping boughs of firs by the beaver dam was white.
Nor did she insist I see her as a girl from an illustrated storybook
Who loved to read by the fire, cook with her mother, and sing
As much as walk in the woods. But I was welcome to see her
Walking through the dappled shade of birch, oak, and maple
With her two brothers, blue jeans cuffed and torn at the knee,
Hay-colored braids bobbing on her sun-freckled shoulders,
A tin pail swinging at her side like a bell. I was free to see them
Skirt the rim of a cellar hole and pass through a gap
In a stone wall, near the crest of a hill, and come out in a clearing
To a rash of ripe blackberries with long strands of thorns
They had to part carefully to pick lest they scratch up their hands.

Told other stories, I might have pictured a placid lake
Or a choppy bay behind her, giving definition to the distance.
Either backdrop could have done her justice, if that's what she'd wanted.
She might have said that when they were done picking blackberries
They continued along the ridge to an outcropping of rock
Where blueberries grew. I would have been happy to see her
Crouching to the low-bush blueberries that grow in the cracks
Of fractured schist and granite boulders, to hear her crunch
Flakes of lichen with each step or shift of her weight.
Truth be told, I would have loved to see her cup her left hand
Beneath a cluster of bell-shaped blueberries, giving it a tug
Until it yielded three or four berries for the pail at a pull.
And later, back in the kitchen of the white colonial saltbox house,
I would have been happy to admire the view of Mount Monadnock
Through one of the nine panes in the north-facing window
While she rolled out the dough for pies she'd put in the oven
Before her mother came in from picking greens in the garden.

But she gave me a first impression, and I have taken it from there.

Earth Day

Now that we'd dug a hole deep enough for the root ball
Of the hawthorn tree that would fill it; now that the two nice guys
In the big orange Department of Public Works pick-up truck
Had shoveled compost into it; now that we'd helped
The arborist place the tree upright in the hole like a flag; and now
That we'd finished spreading compost around its base
And were leaning on our rakes with smiles on our faces,

It was a pleasure, in that residential block of Highland Street
Between Maverick and Central Streets on Bellingham Hill
In Chelsea, overlooking Eagle Hill and Logan International
Airport in East Boston, across the mouths of the Mystic River
And Chelsea Creek in Boston Harbor, right precisely there,
Between the gray granite curb and a mortared stone wall
In front of a house with a cement stoop and vinyl siding,

To hear Eric, the gentle, young, and good-looking arborist
From the Greening the Gateway Cities division
Of the Department of Resource Conservation in Boston,
Furrowing his brow and frowning with feigned embarrassment,
Explain to a curious teenager there with her classmates
From a task force on environmental justice at the nonprofit,
La Colaborativa, that was instrumental in keeping the community

Of Chelsea fed and vaccinated throughout the pandemic,
In response to her question about the gender of the tree,
That, come to think of it, he couldn't actually remember offhand
Whether hawthorns like this, famous for their fragrant flowers,
Were *monoecious*, gender-specific, binary trees that exist
As sexual complements, "and by complements," he said,
"I mean symbiotic opposites, not flattering remarks spelled

With an *i*," that depend, for reproductive success,
On butterflies and bees to deliver the fertile pollen in summer
From the ovulating flower of a tree of the opposite gender,
Or whether they're *dioecious*, hermaphroditic trees instead
With bisexual flowers, and therefore can be considered,
As another teenager huddled around the tree well with Eric
And her classmates pointed out—all of them the children

Of refugees who fled the endemic poverty and gang violence
In the conservative Catholic and evangelical Christian countries
Of Honduras, Guatemala, and El Salvador, in the Northern Triangle—
Code-switching from accented English to colloquial Spanish
And hip-hop Spanglish in her one remarkable, multivalent sentence,
With her reddish-brown skin, her jet-black hair, her cool sneakers,
And her silkscreened t-shirt, as models of a gender identity,

Fluid and nonbinary and confusing to the conventional
Hetero-normative values, that a surprising number of people
Have recently been experimenting with, even here in Chelsea,
Where a woman named Peg, who'd crossed the Tobin Bridge with friends
From a task force on poverty at the Church of the Covenant
In the exclusive Back Bay, to the delight of everyone there
Confirmed on her phone that the hawthorn is, indeed, a nonbinary tree.

Screech Owl

What do you suppose remains of the screech owl this summer
That I returned, last winter, to its original resting grounds
Along the littered tracks where I found it the fall before?
Several heavy snows and rains have fallen since I tossed it

Underhand so softly that I barely heard it settle
In the tangled undergrowth of stalks and rooted weeds.
By now I imagine its feathers have started to show that weather,
As even rocks and the hardened features of humans will,

First by fraying, next by matting, then by detaching altogether
And rising with the wind that dried and picked them up.
But when I found it, the owl hadn't yet had to endure
The first thaw, the one that marks the passage

Of a winged mythical soul from a lower division of heaven
To a higher celestial one. Wings furled, staring head cocked
To its left a little, the owl lay frozen along the parallel rails
That splice the shortest path between the glittering river

And here. Even in death, its curled talons clutched a branch
Or sank into a squirrel's neck. I cringed lifting it
By brown tailfeathers for the quick walk home to the freezer.
Then, for more than a year, I pulled the screech owl's carcass

From among the cartons of ice cream on a whim
For instant meditation, or for amusing a friend over for supper.
I didn't suspect that I was disturbing the natural order
More than the natural order was disturbed already.

I just assumed that a cargo train had knocked it down
From flight one night, caught it on the fly, and carried it into town
Atop a closed boxcar or some heavy freight strapped
With chain to a flatbed. That was the most elemental

Explanation for this phenomenon that I could contrive.
The birds you see around here drift in the water, swing
On window feeders, clutter eaves and granite gutters,
Hop tablet stones in isolated graveyards, or tune up for summer

On rooftop antennae. Merganser ducks, herring gulls,
White geese, and grebes. Sparrows, finches, and chickadees.
Pigeons and starlings. Mockingbirds and cowbirds. Cardinals
And warblers and juncos and catbirds. Even the occasional

Red-tailed hawk is seen soaring above a Sunday park,
Leaving predominantly owls and their love of the dark to remain
Loyal to the country, with farm boys who grow up to raise
The great great grandcalves of their grandfathers' cows.

The Trees of Heaven

Like it or not, ailanthus trees proliferated in this neighborhood
Before gentrification, as scraggly and numerous as the children
Of the Irish-, Portuguese-, and Italian-Americans
Whose families had lived here since the 19th century—
As plentiful, I mean, as the snickering kids who loitered
On the stoops of triple-deckers that the city had built
To accommodate all of the poor Catholic families
Migrating from Europe with the mandate always
To "go forth and multiply" their broods of hungry children.

Called *trees of heaven* in the Asian nations of their origin,
They took advantage of every innocuous opportunity
To prove their adaptability—the females, especially,
Casting on the wind the pungent stench of their fecundity
For a week every June, dropping sex-crazed clusters of blossoms
Onto sidewalks, rooftops, and streets, sending up shoots
From every patch of godforsaken earth, even those pocked
With pumice-like coal cinders from the obsolete furnaces
They heated all the houses with well into the 60s.

And that's how it was until the professionals moved in
With their melancholic babies, their dark mahogany
Antique furniture, their slick wardrobes from Bauhaus boutiques,
And their heavy cultural baggage from seven generations
Of important American personages—planting this greenery,
Marking the hard borders between their renovated properties
With gingko trees and locusts, river birches, hollies,
And moody English yews, prettifying the gravel walkways
Of their perennial Zen gardens with herbs, shrubs, and ivies,
And adorning the intimate dooryards and stoop-side patios
Of their formerly very homely triple-decker houses
With azalea, viburnum, lilac, and suburban rhododendron.

But some of these trees of heavenly origin,
As scrappy as those teens in platoons of six or seven
Who jangled swing sets in underfunded playgrounds
And brooded in public-housing doorways and bleak city parks,
Drawing water from underground pipes, sluiced by drains,
Took such tenacious root along the ubiquitous wire fences

Which the residents collectively hired some outfit to install
Against the crime-wave of the 60s—plumbers and secretaries,
Carpenters and nurses, sailors and sales clerks, proud
To own their own homes after the Second World War—
Still remain, their elephant-gray trunks gaining
Such incredible girth that they have actually engulfed
Sections of those fences, so that a four-foot length of fence,
In a kind of no-man's land between two "developed properties,"
At one time connected to the entire maze of fencing,
Can still be seen in the gray bark of a tree, threading in
And out of the surface of the bark, its diamond weave
Of rust-orange aluminum as visible as a scar in the flesh
Of someone's trunk, like zipper-like stitching left hanging
In the soft skin of someone's torso after a procedure
Where a hernia was corrected, open heart surgery
Was performed, or an appendix, a gallstone, or a tumor
Was removed by a surgeon in a routine emergency.

4

Plumbing

I had to wonder, standing on a cement embankment
Of a dredged canal on a gray British day near Victoria Square,
That if this wasn't what the city of his birth looked like before
It was bombed to smithereens by the Luftwaffe of the Nazis,
With shopping arcades, apartment towers, and pubs that serve
Fish and chips, vegan shepherd's pie, and mushroom burgers
On the foundations of the ruins of the numerous mills,
Then how much uglier could Birmingham have been
When W.H. Auden, the founding former director
Of the Age of Anxiety—who sat, on the first of September,
In 1939, "uncertain and afraid," in a dive on 52nd Street
In New York City, on the eve of the Second World War
Across the pond in Europe—was growing up here, the privileged
But conscientious son of some established professor
Of technology or other, and a public poet of no small significance
Who, not coincidentally, given the city's industrial history,
Was socialist in response to the problems of modernity, including
The blatant exploitation of workers, the dominion
Of corporate bureaucracy, and the specter of mass poverty
That had haunted him since the collapse of the global economy,
Once "the rhetorician's lie/Burst like a pipe" in him, as he said
It had in Rimbaud, the *enfant terrible* of the Symbolist
Late nineteenth century, in the only convincing comparison
Between plumbing and poetry that I have ever come across.

Injunction

Near a storefront *halal* cafe that would serve them lentil soup,
Chicken and lamb shish-kabob, copper pots of mint tea,
And desserts made of honey, flour, pistachios, and ghee
At sundown when the worshippers broke their daylong fasts,
We watched them coming and going, the Pakistani Muslims
Of the new diaspora created by Al-Qaeda and the Taliban
With the help of self-interested American intervention.

From a broken bench in a dusty park on the north side
Of Birmingham, in the hardscrabble district of Aston
Where refugees from less conservative formerly colonial nations
In the West Indies and West Africa also happened to live
With those who fled Partition after India won its freedom,
We watched them, the men in skullcaps and long white *thobes*,
The women in shimmering *saris* and homely *hijabs*
Like those we'd seen on mannequins in a storefront window.

Near a tiled mosque with a gold dome and a cement foundation,
Among gunpowder-gray surroundings, we watched them,
Extended families of multiple generations moving as one,
Their dark-eyed children skipping along the fractured sidewalk
And singing rhymes in Urdu that we imagined had to do
With the love of Allah and the joys of fasting and feasting.

We watched them all, the masses of Muslim people,
Among them those more likely to speak Arabic than Urdu,
Driven from their homes in Syria, Iraq, and Yemen, too,
By the civil strife resulting from Sunni and Shia division,
Quiet, blameless, and modest, living it up for Ramadan.

Among them were several young observant women
Whom we might have mistaken for Malala Yousafzai,
A resident of Birmingham since being taken there for treatment
After a nearly successful attempt on her life by an assassin
Back home in the Swat Valley of northwestern Pakistan,
Winner of the Nobel Prize for Peace for openly defying
The injunction against education for Islamic girls and women.

And while we watched them, these masses of migrants
From colonies formed by the British after the First World War,
We thought of that other injunction, quoted so often
Since 9/11, that W.H. Auden, a Birmingham native, placed
At the end of his poem "September 1, 1939," on the eve
Of World War Two, to wit: *We must love one another or die—*
Even if he regretted it later, and even if he agreed,
At the request of some persuasive editor, albeit too late
To keep the original from entering the canon, to let
The poem be reprinted only if the optional conjunction
In that final line were changed not to the defiant but
But to the democratic and neutral conjunction *and.*

We must love one another and die—love one another and die!

At the Childhood Home of Ozzy Osbourne

At 15 Lodge Road, around the corner from a long stretch
Of grim gray "council housing" apartment complexes
That shelter vulnerable refugees from places torn to pieces
By the nail-stuffed bombs of angry fundamentalist warriors,

At a crook in the lane where the rock 'n' roll celebrity star
Of his own reality television show, the notorious Ozzy Osbourne,
First conceived of those blasphemously loud Black Sabbath songs
Of an unintentionally funny, head-banging quality

That marked the heavy metal hey-day of the early 1970s,
We happen upon the loyal, long-time neighbors
Still holding out in their scruffy and contaminated
Working-class element, their urban-slum enclave,

The elderly white Anglo gal with the fresh blue hairdo
And the dreadlocked Jamaican dude on the blue sting-ray bike,
Cataloguing the changes that have come in recent years
To this very humble neighborhood where Ozzy came up

As a blue-collar Brummie, in the borough of Aston
On the north side of Birmingham, north of the mills
That William Blake derided, far from the Bournville hill
With the Cadbury chocolate plant and the complex of cottages

And sweet little townhouses on the south side of town
That the Quaker capitalist who owned that business
Had built to keep his workers productive and happy—
Cataloguing the changes that have come in recent years

And complaining aloud that since the Pakistanis' arrival
It isn't any longer the peaceful mixture of dour Anglos
And mellow West Indians that it used to be,
That it no longer embodies the unlikely alliance of people

That made it a model of cross-cultural possibility,
Where an unexpected blend of black and white Marleys,
Those descended, like him, from the Bobs of Rastafarian fame
And those descended, like her, from the Jacobs of Dickens's

Christmas Carol acclaim, could treat each other with dignity
As they are doing now, these loyal, long-time neighbors,
At the door of the rock star's home, this bland gray
Cement-block townhouse from whose picture window comes,

Not as if out of nowhere, but out of the depths of hell,
As we are about to ask if they knew Ozzy in person,
The sound of a man in a rage letting his frustration out
In Urdu, Pashto, or Punjab, screaming bloody murder

At someone in his family who's been stuck with him at home
For too damn long in those uncomfortably close quarters
Whimpering behind a closed door, cowering in a corner,
Hiding behind the bathroom door, or standing ground

Before him in the kitchen. His rebellious son, maybe.
His longsuffering wife, perhaps. Or, if it has come to that,
His disappointed mother, who's been nagging him all summer
To get off his duff, get off the dole, and get some sort

Of job for a change. Whatever it takes to make him feel
Proud about something, for Allah's almighty sakes,
Like he did back home when he and his brother had
That successful little recycling business, back in big Islamabad.

The Sonnet

Initially, after reading that title, "To the River Otter,"
At the top of the page in the Coleridge collection,
I didn't realize that the poem would be addressed
To the river instead of the otter. That would come later.

For now, I inferred in a studious glance
At the irregularly rhyming end-word of each
Of the fourteen lines of iambic pentameter
That the poem lacked the three regulation quatrains
With alternating rhyme schemes, abab, cdcd, efef,
And a concluding gg couplet that are characteristic
Of a Shakespearean sonnet, and that it also didn't have
The octave-sestet structure of the Petrarchan.

Between two blinks of my eyes, before I started reading,
I wondered what the poet would say to the otter
In a dense apostrophe typical of even the most
Irregular approximation of a formal sonnet
With an erratic scheme, *abbaa cdcdcd ece,*
That keeps you guessing the rhyme that comes next.

*

Would he dare say, "Oh sleek inhabitant of freshwater pools,
Is it true that you dive for fun as well as for fish!"?

Would he address one of the cute aquatic creatures
With the torso of a beaver and the face of a dog
That he'd seen on a ramble with Dorothy and William
Along the Wye, near the border of Wales and England,
Or in that other much-favored place, along the Kent
In the Lake District, on a summer day in the 1790s,
When *Lyrical Ballads* was about to be published—

Like the one we saw while canoeing on the same Concord
River that Thoreau and his brother spent a week on
In the 1830s, after their week on the Merrimac
In southern New Hampshire, or like the ones we admired
From the shore of Shell Pond in Evans Notch that other time,

Sliding across the border of Maine and New Hampshire
Toward the fishing hole they'd clawed in the ice,
Two otters waiting as the next in line got traction,
Waddled on its webbed feet as fast as it could,
And plunged in with a splash, before climbing out
Of the same hole in the ice to get in line again?

*

Would there be mention of the men being oblivious
To the otter at first, clasping their soft scholarly hands
Behind them as they walked, fixing their bright eyes
To the stony ground, engrossed in their discussion
Of the composition of conversational poems in blank verse,
Discussing the effects of breaking a poetic line
Between the adjective and the noun that it modifies,
Or between one indispensable prepositional
Phrase and another; of the pleasures of tripping
The poem's rhythm with a reversed iambic foot
Starting a line, and of enjambing lines like this one
To surprise and delight the expectations of the reader,
Or the application of the elements of prosody
To the newly awakened sense of the life of the body,
Branded taboo since the arrival of Christianity,
William, by way of illustration, beginning to recite
"Resolution and Independence," with its adaptation,
However brief, of overheard common speech
To formal meter, claiming, with regard to the leech-gatherer,
That "the whole body of the Man did seem
Like one whom I had met with in a dream,"
When all of a sudden Dorothy, linen-sleeved arms
Folded at her bosom, began to show that shock
Of recognition we know by the gaping mouth
And the in-drawn exclamation, on seeing the black nose
And the V-shaped ripple of white bubbles behind it
That meant the otter was darting with a *swoosh*
Toward the other side of the Wye or the Kent
From the reeds in the marshes like a slow-motion arrow?

*

When the otter disappeared into the reeds
On the other bank, I figured they'd set their knapsacks down,
Unpack the loaf of bread, the wedge of cheddar, the bottle
Of port wine, and start to enjoy their picnic right there,
As happily out of sorts as the otter with the timeclocks,
Smokestacks, and kitschy little Christmas knick-knacks
Of the Industrial Revolution that was up and running
In Birmingham, Manchester, and London by then,
At ease in the shade of a plane tree with big green leaves
And layers of dark gray and pale green outer bark
Peeling away like jigsaw pieces from the pale inner bark
That protects the camber from insects and birds.

But when I read the invocation in the first line
Of the Coleridge sonnet—*Dear native brook! wild streamlet of the West!*—
And the bit about skimming a "smooth thin stone"
Along the surface when he was just "a careless child"—
When "willows gray" grew on the shore of the brook,
When the "bedded sand" was "veined with various dyes"

And "[g]eamed" through the water's "bright transparence"—
I understood that the poet, employing a word-order
Unlike that in the colloquial adaptation of common speech
To free verse "in plain American which cats and dogs"
In the Marianne Moore poem can read, wasn't really talking
To an otter after all, but to the river they named it after,
The River Otter, which, according to footnotes, flowed
Through the Blackdown Hills of England, in Somerset County,
A nominal river preceding an adjectival otter in a riff
On an 18th century tradition of apostrophes to rivers.

In the Southern-Most Mexican State of Chiapas

In San Cristóbal de las Casas, the center of the dioceses run
By the sixteenth century critic of the conquistadors' brutal
Mistreatment of the Indians, *Bartolomé de las Casas*,
In the southern-most Mexican state of Chiapas,
We had been in conversation, in a remarkably easy Spanish,
For a good twenty minutes, with the affable and handsome agent
At his *turismo* office, around the corner from our sweet posada,
Assuring him, *por supuesto, sí sí sí,* while he arranged our return
To Boston via Tuxtla Gutierrez, the capital city
An hour and a half away, that we had been enjoying
The cafes and historical sites in the picturesque colonial quarter
Before and after visiting the monkeys and the toucans
In the Maya jungle ruins at magnificent Palenque;
That we had patronized the market in the yard of the cathedral,
Eating mangos with pepper and lime, *elotes* (corn on the cob),
And quesadillas *con hongos y nopales*, mushrooms and cactus,
For lunch every day; that we'd visited the *hacienda*
Of the wealthy anthropologists who championed the rights
Of the indigenous people in the Laconda jungle
Near the border of Guatemala for most of their long lives;
And that we'd even done the tour of the San Juan Chamula village
To watch a priest in a white tunic roll an egg along the limbs
Of a pregnant young woman, wand her with a Coke bottle,
And bless her with an incantatory prayer spoken in *Tuitil,*
Among the hundreds of Virgin of Guadalupe *veladoras*
Flickering among pine boughs on the tile floor of the church—

Testimonies from a paradise that seemed to disappear
When he asked if we had heard, on our walk to that village
With self-appointed guide Roberto, who apparently considered this
Something he should hide, about the recent assassination
Of Chamula's corrupt mayor, Domingo López, and all but one
Of his complicit councilors, on an ordinary weekday morning
Just three weeks before, right there on the zócalo, right there
On the town square, in front of the same church
Where we'd witnessed that blessing, in sight of and in spite of
Its heavenly blue and white trim, its symbolic decals
On cornices and door frames, after three urgent warnings,
A death threat or two, and an ultimatum from the representative

Of the craftswomen's union to cough up the funds
That the collective had applied for the year before and won
From the federal government, for the further development
Of their folk-art crafts business, in the artesanía, in the open air.

Roberto himself had been more than memorable, walking us
All the way up the road from San Cristóbal to Chamula
On his one day off from busing dishes at a four-star hotel,
Slugging shots of moonshine *pox*, pronounced to rhyme with *slosh*,
From a repurposed Fanta bottle, then letting us treat him
To the house special (grilled meats on pasta) and two cervezas
At a taqueria adjacent to the graveyard of his parents
Before breaking into a rain dance to recorded marimba
While a caged parrot chattered raucous accusations in Spanish
And a thunderstorm drum-rolled the fiberglass roof.

But no! we said. ¡*No hemos escuchado ni una palabra de eso*!
We hadn't heard a word about the murder on the *zócalo*.
And yes, we had enjoyed our visit to the museum of Maya
Medicine on that side street on the outskirts of the capital.

*

For me, it was all I could do, standing at the thresholds
Of the museum's softly lit galleries, to keep from jumping
The velvet rope, to suppress the surging, atavistic desire
To enter each astonishing diorama and surrender myself
To the depicted scene, taking my place among
The lifelike wax figures in one after another vignette
Of people in imaginable action—to join the life-sized,
Round-shouldered, black-haired indigenous women
Weaving wool clothing on looms in thatched huts,
Grinding maize on stone mortars, flipping tortillas
On rocks over pine-wood fires, and worshipping the gods
Of corn, rain, sunlight, and fertility with their husbands,
Their children, their extended families of grandparents
And cousins, on their hut's dirt floor, cushioned by a bed
Of fresh pine needles, like those we'd seen at the cathedral

On the *zócalo* in San Juan Chamula, where that priest
In a long white tunic, blessing that young woman,
Chanted that prayer in his staccato *Tuitil*, rolled an egg
Along her limbs, and wanded her with a full bottle
Of Coca-Cola, aglow in the light of hundreds of candles
Flickering in glass cups on the tile floor until
His cell phone rang and he excused himself for a minute—

"Or not just to join," I joked, "but actually to be the man
In draw-string white pants and brown leather sandals,
Right about my size, someone I'm sure I could emulate,"
His black hair square on his head, cutting firewood
In a clearing with a homemade axe, bare-chested and brown
As the man in the adjacent gallery thatching his hut
With palm leaves and lengths of vine, happy at last
To be as soft as that, no longer a perishable man
Of warm blood and brittle bone, *hueso y carne*, subject
To all sorts of suffering, worried about the world,
No longer to be concerned about my mortality or reputation,
But content with my life, busy at last at the kind of hard work
That keeps you attached without twine to the earth.

*

But before we saw any of the actual exhibitions,
In the company of three other tourists whose plain looks
And archaeology books belied the warm demeanors
They'd cultivated for years at Midwestern universities,
We'd watched an introductory, 10-minute video about
The natural healing arts that to this day are practiced
In the remote, tropical-rainforest villages of Laconda
Along the steamy border with equally Maya Guatemala,
Squinting, from folding chairs in the foyer, with our daypacks
And our bottles of *agua purificada*, at an old Motorola
Monitor they'd planted on a foot stool, at the grainy,
Anthropological, sixteen-millimeter documentary footage
Of a midwife in braids and *huipil* working to bring a baby forth
In the traditional way, kneeling, to our surprise, *behind*
The upright, expectant mother, with a pail of water

And a knife that had been sterilized over the same open fire
They cooked their stews and tortillas on, preparing to cut
The umbilical cord, the laboring woman leaning forward
At the waist from her standing position, by golden candlelight
On the dirt floor of the thatched hut in the middle of the night
Pushing and grunting and parting her thighs a little more,
Holding onto her stone-faced husband for support and dear life.

*

As the affable agent printed out our tickets, we listed
The native medicinal plants we read about on the poster board,
The foam-core chart, on a typewritten spreadsheet,
In the last gallery we visited in the medicine museum—
Jalapeño, cacao, pitarilla, agave, romero, y tobaco—along
With the ailments they can cure, from sexual dysfunction,
Gastrointestinal distress, and kidney, liver, and heart ailments,
To emotional trauma, if prepared from the original
Homeopathic recipes that, according to the indignant caption
Posted on the wall beneath each corresponding sample
Of dried herbal remedy, have been confiscated from
The famously biodiverse jungles of Laconda
By specimen-gathering scientists who bring them back north
And develop them synthetically, under lucrative contract
With pharmaceutical companies like Lilly and Merck,
In sterile stainless-steel biomedical research laboratories
Connected at the pelvis to well-endowed universities
Like those in the glass towers, the architectural prize winners
That line both sides of Main Street like the walls of a canyon,
Where candy factories, diners, and retail shops used to be,
Back home, on the other side of Central Square, up there
In Cambridge, near the massive campus of the Massachusetts
Institute of Technology, more than two thousand miles
From the camouflaged jaguar that stalks the two unwary
North American scientists in pith helmets, blue shirts, boots,
And tan khakis, in foliage growing over the glyphic ruins
Of an ancient stone house, in the mural we saw, back
By the *baños*, for *damas* and *caballeros*, on our way out the door.

Tag

Done giving directions in a stilted textbook Spanish
That the tourists can understand, done closing out the register
Of pesos devalued to the equivalent of our dimes, and done
Stocking the towering racks with dictionaries, maps,
And picture-postcard views of the monogamous volcanoes
Of Mesoamerican myth that we have seen from certain
Perspectives in town—smoking-hot snow-cone Popo
And his jagged wife Itzy—the pretty young women
Who run the information booth in the town of Tlaxcala
Are rolling down the corrugated blinds, turning off the lights,
Blowing each other their *buenas noches* kisses, and going their ways
Down the narrow colonial avenues radiating like the spokes
Of a wheel from the fountain in the hub of the *zócalo*.

The one with glasses, we just know, will join her family
For guacamole, quesadillas, refritos, and menudo
In the kitchen of an apartment connected to the tortilla shop
That they named for Juan Diego, the 16th century Aztec man
Who envisioned the Virgin Mary as an indigenous woman;
The one with the limp will head to the pavilion beside the canal
At the foot of the hill, where her parents sell tropical fruit—
Bananas, papayas, and mangos—from table-top pyramids modeled
After those at Teotihuacan, the complex that resembles most
The Pentagon, in an aisle as long as *la Calle de los Muertos*,
Where fried grasshopper and *chicharrone* pork rind
Both can be found. And the one with long legs, crossing that canal
On a stone bridge and climbing the hill, will go to the school
In the basement of the church we've seen on the cliff from below,
To pick up her sister after work like she does every day.

She'll go straight up the hill, along the cactus fences guarding
The small garden plots of the pastel houses, where vines
Of magenta bougainvillea braid all the drainpipes,
Below the barking mongrels patrolling all the patios.
Taking a right, just past the last house at the crest of the hill,
She'll walk between cornfields in a cobblestone lane
To the church on the cliff, where a graveyard comes into view.

She'll see a line of little girls begin to meander toward her
From the cliff when they see her; she'll see them suspend
Their game of tag to admire her up close, visible only as black
Silhouettes against the sky at first. But then they'll emerge
From the aisles of the graveyard, with their black tresses streaming
Behind them like flags, and their cotton dresses white
Against their reddish-brown complexions, to gather in a line
Along the wall of the cemetery to greet the older sister
Of the beautiful little fleet-footed girl who is "it" until,
Catching up with her classmates at the wall, she makes the look
Of apprehension curl at both ends of her big sister's lips
Into a smile of recognition that also shifted her hips.

5

Barrio Boston

Halfway back to the home of Néstor and Consuelo
On Eighteenth Street, *Calle Diez y Ocho*, among
The street-corner *arepa* stands, the stacked rowhouses,
And the storefront *panederías* of Barrio San Luís,
I'd reached that stretch of road where the numerous *motos*,
Rattling diesel trucks, frequent local buses, and dozens
Of dented yellow taxis with more efficient engines
All blow blue smoke into the otherwise fragrant
Andean mountain air. In the seismic city of Pereira,
On the slopes of Nevado del Ruiz, in the dramatic
Eje cafetero, the "coffee axis" of Colombia,
In the volcanic agricultural region in the central
Cordillera, I was almost as far as that dilapidated,
Drab, cement-block convenience store
Called, to my New Englander's surprise, *Kiosko Boston*,
Near a picturesque warren of ramshackle shelters
On the bank of a raunchy *barranco* below, a rank
Residential ravine like those I'd seen in Guatemala,
Where people prop their corrugated roofing sheets
Of fiberglass up with walls of sticks and blocks.
And I was glancing around with the same curiosity
As that of the seven or eight dusty yellow canaries
That had just landed in the diamond-shaped gaps
Of a chain-link fence protecting a precious lot of rubble,
Near a mango tree that was defying all convention
By bearing fruit in spite of all the contamination,
When I saw him up ahead, a man I swore I'd seen
On those same streets of Guatemala before, if not on those
Of Puerto Rico, Ecuador, Mexico, and El Salvador.

Scrawny and scrappy, in synthetic work clothes that looked
Like part of his actual body, a bronzed brown blur
Of sensuous creases and folds, he had risen from the ground
With an enormous bouquet of tropical flowers held
Like a rifle on his shoulder. I saw assorted species
Of bromeliad and heliconia. There was a bird of paradise
With orange petals flaming from the red and gold sepals
Like candlesticks on the pole of an acolyte's torch
Along the three green branches that extended from the stalk.

In a hurry to get back, I wouldn't have broken stride
If I hadn't noticed that he had knocked to the ground
The ballcap he wore to keep the sun out of his eyes
On his way back up from kneeling down to tie his shoes,
From buckling a notch or two tighter the belt he used
To keep his trousers from falling without warning
To his ankles, from wiping his brow, and from taking a sip
Of water from a Fanta bottle. I would have kept going
Like the dusty-yellow canaries that just then took flight.

Without hesitation, moving into action, surrendering
To it even, as if choreographed, programmed,
And destined to do it, as if born to lend a hand
To this inconspicuous man, I took the steps necessary
In his direction. I knelt to retrieve the cap, that is,
That had landed with an almost visible sound
On the peripheral ground, in three descending steps
Bending into a crouch in the brown powdered dust
Between a red candy wrapper and a gold lottery ticket
That some poor working stiff who dreamt of quitting
His job stocking shelves at the *supermercado*
And buying a finca near the the hot-spring *termales*
Above the nearby pueblo of Santa Rosa had discarded.
Grabbing the hat by the bill, I followed through
On the exhale, as if working through an *asana*
In a yoga class back home, rising from the same crouch
That he had just arisen from, swiveling my head
In its own tight ballcap, looking up and into the umber
Features of his gaunt face, into his caramel-colored eyes
And his thin, toothless grin, and handing it to him
With a ceremonious smile, that hat mass-produced
In China, Ghana, India, Brazil, or Vietnam,
And monogrammed with the logo, a jaguar or a puma,
Of some dumb conglomerate, like Dow or Monsanto,
That sells pesticides and disease-resistant seeds
To flower farms and coffee plantations in the fertile valley
Around the volcano, in doing so clarifying for now
With unconditional love my confusion about the world.

When he nodded *Gracias* and went on his way
Up the busy thoroughfare, between the mall on his left
And the depot on his right, toward the hilltop *centro*,
I just stood there, certain that he could sell those flowers,
Scavenged from the compost heap of some big *vivera*
Behind the long greenhouses on the outskirts of the city,
If not at high-end prices to well-dressed designers
At air-conditioned warehouses near the airport
Who'd trim their stalky stems and steep them with ferns
In deep glass vases, for placement on the steps
Of elegant public spaces, in the vaulted lobbies
Of restaurants and banks, department stores and malls,
Then for next to nothing to a housekeeping woman
From a barrio better than Boston on the outskirts of town
On her way back, say, to the bus stop with her bags
Looking for something to brighten up the foyer
Or the kitchen table, at the end of her daily marketing.

Athens County Breakdown

Just outside of the tiny village of Amesville, which
The children of pioneers who'd crossed the Ohio River
From Virginia had settled in spite of its poor drainage
More than a century before, sat that big square house
That Will Dewees rented out to classmates of ours
While he was on leave from his job at the university—
Jerry and Deb in a room upstairs, Linda and her daughter
In another, Jim downstairs, and Donny in the cabin out back.

With its detached summer kitchen, its limestone foundation,
Its faded grandeur, and its setting on the creek,
Connected to the road by a bridge of tied logs,
It reminded me a lot of a Yoknapatawpha County setting
In a short story or novel by the inimitable William Faulkner—
Major de Spain's place in "Barn Burning," say, featuring
The notorious Abner Snopes, the antebellum house built
By Thomas Sutpen in *Absalom, Absalom!*, or the doomed abode
Of the Compson family in *The Sound and the Fury*.
At least it did later—after I'd actually read that stuff.

Our shelter, though, the makeshift one that Phil and I shared,
Just a shack, really, a cheap box of aluminum sheets
From the lithographic print shop of the *Columbus Dispatch*
That Will and friends had learned to nail to two-by-fours
On a volunteer project they'd done in East Africa
To make perfectly serviceable, if temporary, lodgings,
On the slope of a ridge overlooking the fallow field
That filled a narrow flood plain between a parallel ridge
And ours, was set back another one hundred yards or so
From the gravel road and the creek that ran along it.

The silver rectangular sheets of aluminum on the wall
Still bore headlines from past editions of the paper
That we could read again, hanging out at our only table
With a view of the field through the Plexiglass window—

Not news we might have read back in the 1860s
About the rippled region across that great river
Seceding from the Secessionists and becoming West Virginia

On the grounds that they had poor agriculture, no
Aristocracy to speak of, and nothing to gain from slavery,
But news from the turbulent late 1960s
And the early 1970s that now were fresh history.

Johnson's decision, in light of the opposition
To his program in Vietnam, not to run for President again;
Nixon and Kissinger's infamous Christmas Day surprise
Bombing of Cambodia; the Manson Family massacre
Of Hollywood celebrities. Traffic accidents. Box scores.
And endless reports on the Watergate hearings.

Not that we ever did that, really—except for momentary
Amusement as we swilled our Rolling Rock beer
Or sipped from ceramic mugs our weak Folgers coffee.

*

Not having met him more than once or twice, I don't know
How it was for Will, growing up in the 40s and 50s
In the suburbs of Chicago, according to his obituary,
And returning from service in international development,
To go back to the land like that, and to start himself both
An intentional community and a daffodil business—
Nor, for that matter, how it was for Jerry and Deb,
He from Dayton and she from a suburb of Boston,
Lusty young lovers who had each other for breakfast;
For countercultural blue-collar mountain mama Linda
And her barefoot daughter running around in her underwear;
For tall and slender Jim, the keeper of egg-laying geese
Who was particularly fond of Jesse Colin Young's song
"Hippie from Olema," a send-up of the Merle Haggard tune
That begins, "I'm proud to be an Okie from Muskogee";
And for Donny in the cabin at the head of the holler,
Determined, like Jim, to go to law school to defend us
Against the wily capitalists who've since taken over.

But for a flatlander like me from a white bread suburb
On the outskirts of Columbus, grandson to natives
Of Old McDonald farms and German Village bakeries, son
Of sheet-metal fabricator and pink-collar worker,
It was a rare thrill to live out there, on the rustic backroads
Of rural Amesville, especially in that improvised shack
On the side of even the most utterly insignificant hill
With loyal friend Phil—the curious and capable son
Of an architect and a doctor from a suburb of Cleveland.

I loved that it was built on four stilts of two-by-fours,
And that a brook trickled beneath it on its way downhill,
In ironic homage to Frank Lloyd Wright's *Falling Water*.
With no telephone or plumbing, with natural gas siphoned
From an oil claim on the property, and with electricity run,
Illegally, by buried wire from the main house on the road,
Where we had access to the toilet and the shower,
That place put me closer than ever to the weather.

*

Sometimes, climbing to the ridge top, following the creek
Beyond Donny's cabin, which he, Phil, and classmates
In a Foxfire program had moved to the holler,
Or throwing sticks for my dog between the barn and the house,
I wondered whether, like certain iconic figures
Of eastern religious legend, I could dissolve myself in nature
And immerse my consciousness so selflessly in the imagery
That, for all intents and purposes, my identity would disappear,
Or at least the reprehensible aspects of my character.

At other times, living in the boonies of Athens County
Was enough to drive me to write the kind of poetry
That those same ethereal luminaries might have written
As concession and consolation when the revelation failed
And they needed to do something quick to get it back.

Not the poems lamenting an unrequited infatuation,
Comparing greater Columbus to a gigantic ant colony,
And worrying about the environmental implications
Of my black VW bug, but those I recorded in my journal
When a male cardinal, flying across the stubble
Of that fallow field in fall, showed off its scarlet crest,
When an ice-white blizzard huffed and puffed and tried
To blow the flimsy shack down, when mayflower and dogwood
Bloomed in the woods, and when the creek rose so high
With cold spring rain that it flooded the shallow valley,
Washing out our bridge, scattering its skinned logs,
Stranding cars, tractors, and trucks, and clogging for a week
The village's one commercial block with brush and dead dogs.

Poplar Hollow Inventory

In the George Washington National Forest, partway
From Charlottesville to Columbus, near the border
Of Virginia and West Virginia, in my dire search
For a vicarious and uncomplicated rural existence
That I could inhabit and call my very own
For an hour or two, I parked the compact rental car
In the fossil-like ruts that the letter carrier made
In front of one of the ramshackle houses that I'd been seeing
On state routes and dirt roads in hollers off the highway
Leaning out the window of her big beige Dodge
To fill the metal mailbox with medical and utility bills
Probably never paid on time—bills now scattered
With supermarket circulars in a sloppy concentric ring
On the ground around the base of the mailbox post
Like spent petals fallen from a withered yellow rose
That a woman in a rose-pink apron on a Saturday morning
In summer might have picked from a thorned bush beside
The side door to place in a tall transparent green
Plastic Woolworth vase, on an aquamarine Formica table
In the room I visited first, her yellow-and-white kitchen.

*

After casting a glance at the complete disarray—
Beer cans crushed in the corner, scattered in the pantry,
And piled on the counters, the toaster oven full
Of a mouse's messy nest, the sink to the brim
In porcupine droppings, and the fridge tipped on its side
Like an ancient Roman column—I found a dogeared issue
Of *Ladies' Home Journal* from 1972
On that aquamarine kitchen table by the green Woolworth vase
Open to an article on drunk, dysfunctional husbands
And bookmarked to recipes for cardamom coffee cake
And baked ham with green beans and scalloped potatoes
And knew that's what she must have cooked for dinner
One night per week that winter, in the rose-pink apron
That I now noticed hanging from a hook on the open door
Of a pantry with shelves that were empty but for
A rusted collection of flour, bean, and cornmeal canisters.

*

In the bedroom adjacent to the kitchen, there was more
Useful material for a vicarious existence
That I could adopt for that hour or two, including
The beige nylon slacks and yellow knit sweater she wore
To clerk at the register of the pharmacy or the grocery store,
A black-and-white checkerboard housedress nearly
Eaten off its hanger in a nearby closet by moths,
A few used tubes of dime-store lipstick on a bureau,
"One," she might have said, "for every shade of red
My husband made me see by," and on the wall
Between the creek-facing windows, a framed photograph,
Overlooked when the house was cleared out,
Of her two daughters standing in the front yard
In the shade of a walnut tree, the elder in a black
Nylon cardigan sweater and a subdued expression,
The outgoing younger one in orange braids, plaid blouse,
And orange spray of facial freckles, with a gap between
Her two front teeth, grinning at the camera
In a corduroy jumper, as irrepressibly cheerful
As the candy-stripers hired at the medical clinic in town
To solace the sorrowful kin of the dying.

*

When I found, in a black bin in a corner of the bedroom,
A cowboy hat with a snakeskin band, a court summons
From the county sheriff who pulled him over again
For weaving the line drunk in the winter of 1973,
The brittle sheet music to Volume Three of *Ernest Tubb's
Sensational Successes,* and some misspelled verses in
His own sappy hand, its lyrics in square quatrains
Declaiming in moon-June rhymes a love for the land,
I felt sorry for the jam that I imagined she was in then
After her husband took sick with cirrhosis for good
And she took initiative to move them all to town
To live above that Greyhound, taxi, and Amtrak office run
By Mr. Wood, the science teacher I met the next day

At the station in Clifton Forge (fired, he'd say,
For the accidental poisoning of a chemistry student)
In furnished rooms he let, ordinarily, to C&O
Engineers, porters, conductors, and brakemen
Back before the anthracite from the deep mines first
And then the bituminous too, from hillside strip mines
And mountaintop removal sites, up and quit rolling
Through a region that's been bombed out of its mind
On belts of booze and Bible since the discovery
Of natural gas, fracking, and viscous black petroleum—

But not as sorry as I felt for the broken vanity mirror
In the bathroom adjacent to the bedroom
That her husband used to comb his thick orange curls in,
The left corner of my mouth as visible in the same
Distorted shard of my fragmented reflection
As a wedge of my chin, my left eyebrow alone
In another shard altogether, without my left eye,
Orange seams of rusted metal (more orange, it seems,
Than a family has a right to) showing right through
The cracks in the glass, which must have broken
When they moved away and it realized that no one
Else in the world would ever be able to love it for its mind.

*

On the way out, passing through the shared front corner
Bedroom of the girls—a Wonder Woman doll here,
A plastic houndstooth hairbrush there, and a pee-stained
Mattress on the double bed—I found my way
To the front door hallway, exited with a yank,
And leaned against the front of the house
In a hornbeam wicker chair that I had to right
From the debris of torn screens and rotting lumber
That used to be the front porch, where the daughters,
Hot afternoons, sat in a swing they'd strung
By rope from a limb of the walnut tree, breathing in
The field of clover across the road, the slope
Of tulip poplars rising beyond to the limestone ridge,

And the sun swinging low in the southern sky
As though from the fatigue that they could alleviate
With exaggerated yodels echoing down the holler
Through the orchestra of crickets, locusts, cicadas,
And katydids rubbing their skinny legs together
In a syncopated rhythm the individual elements of which
They could name by tone, pitch, and duration, dangling
Their own skinny legs at the knee from the swing.

Soundtrack

1

Before she did the deed, before she took the rope
And slung it over the pipe in the basement of her building
In Salt Lake City, before she climbed onto the chair,
Slipped the noose around her neck, and kicked
The chair out from under her, she was so incredibly sick
Of the manic depression and the medication she took
To keep the episodes away, that it gave her some relief,
I realize now, twenty years after her death during Y2K,
If she had called at an unexpected hour to say
That the FBI, or the CIA, was gassing her apartment again,
To hear me do my a *cappella* versions of songs we'd heard
At concerts that summer, in June, July, and August, 1976,
When we worked together on the nut-butter line
At the natural foods factory and shared an apartment
In a barrio of Boston—my mock-soulful shout-outs
To Ray Charles rhapsodizing "America the Beautiful"
And the Four Tops choreographing "Bernadette"
In harmony at the stadium in Lynn; my heavy-lidded riff
On the Grateful Dead doing "Brokedown Palace"
And "Box of Rain" at the Orpheum by the Common;
My Caribbean-inflected impersonation of Taj Mahal
Singing "Take a Giant Step" at the Opera House;
Even my take on Tchaikovsky's 1812 Overture
By Arthur Fiedler and the Boston Pops at the bicentennial
Concert on the Charles River Esplanade, which,
Given its rhythmic crescendo, its bombastic celebration
Of military might, the absence of a lip-synch-able libretto,
And the possible confusion that might be caused
By the coincidence of the Russian defense against Napoleon
And the resistance to British aggression led by Oliver Perry
On Lake Erie in the War of 1812, I always saved
For the climactic *ka-boom* of crackling cannonballs
And exploding fireworks from my chest at the end,
Before wishing her a calm evening and signing quietly off.

2

Shifting my hips, and putting the book of Rilke poems
Face-down on the coffee table, I rolled onto my side
And pulled myself up to a sitting position on the futon couch
To answer the phone. It was her again—Jan, seeking comic relief
From the paralyzing effects of the medication.

I thought she might be hoping to hear my impressions
Of the standards that friends from the natural foods warehouse
In the Fort Point section of South Boston played
At that party they threw at their rented Marshfield saltbox
On the bay one humid day, and of the songs we'd seen
Bob Dylan perform, later that night on television,
With the Rolling Thunder Revue, from pillows in their den.

A few minutes into our conversation, I yanked the coiled cord
Of the telephone aside like the cable of a microphone
On a music festival stage, wailed like a *wah-wah* pedal, and whined
Into the receptive receiver like amplifier feedback
From a vintage cherry-red Fender Stratocaster guitar.

Even when we went back to talking, I continued to play
Those solo virtuosic air guitar licks, but silently to myself now
And unbeknownst to her on the line from California,
For the duration of our monthly hourlong conversation,
With the volume of my make-believe amp turned all the way down,
As she reviewed episodes of her serialized love life
In response to my invitation, telling me again
How she'd broken up with that strong but silent Chicano guy,
How her South Asian fiancée had been threatening to leave her
Since she confessed that she wasn't a virgin after all,
And how the guy immediately preceding me back then,
A free-spirited Deadhead hippie, made love with her at the library
In a carrel at UC Santa Cruz in the earlier 1970s.

I couldn't very well continue my parodies on that note—
Mock-orgasmic medley of arias and anti-anthems
With somatic-surrealistic lyrics by The Doors and Jimi Hendrix—

So I put my glib wannabe-rock-star impersonations away
And tried to do my best to listen with full attention
To the terror I heard reverberating behind her every explanation.

And not until I'd done my impersonation of Dylan
By testing my imaginary harmonica against the receiver
With vibrations of my lips, muttering with a caustic snarl
Cryptic criticism of all the people out to exploit me,
And whining my nasal way into that one about the idiot wind
Blowing "from the Grand Coulee Dam to the Capitol"
That we saw Dylan and his motley crew of musicians play
After the two of us returned from watching the sun go down together
From a rowboat moored by chain to a cement block
Among the lily pads and eelgrass across the quiet road
From the saltbox cottage, on the shore of the turgid bay,
Was I able to get her to laugh out loud again.

3

The last time we spoke, she reminded me of the time I posed
For an 18-by-24 watercolor portrait, sitting on a hard chair
In the unfurnished parlor of the triple-decker apartment
We shared with friends from work, on that dead-end street
Abutting Olmsted's Franklin Park in the Puerto Rican barrio
Of Jamaica Plain, in Boston. Surely, I remembered the picture—
My beard still black on my bony chin, the top two buttons
Of my green shirt open, my left hand fretting the thick neck
Of a nylon-stringed, hobo guitar that I'd picked up at a yard sale,
While my right one put a plastic pic to work on a minor chord?

She said I was probably playing, in synch with the crickets chirping
In the puddingstone woods out back, my ardent renditions
Of Bob Dylan songs, bringing to death again, with cramped chord,
Vexed voice, and stiff strum, some ballad of soft seduction
From those love songs Dylan sang when he was in his 20s
As I was with her—or snarling a lyric about the challenges
Of being in love with another complicated, contradictory woman.

"Or maybe you were performing one of those social-justice anthems
About the assassination of Medger Evers, the threat
Of a nuclear holocaust, or the hard rain that had been falling
In your book of sheet music from the earlier Dylan, pretending
That you could put an end to war and segregation, ha ha, and close
The gap between the filthy rich and the dirt poor for good."

"Of course I remember that watercolor portrait you did of me," I said—
"Until last fall, in fact, when my mother died and my father
Tossed it in the trash, sold our house, and moved in with my sister
And her new husband in Dayton, that damn picture hung by a nail
On the block wall of my basement bedroom back home in Ohio."

For all I know, I was humming, hamming, and hymning
An exaggerated nasal rendition of some Beat surrealist twist
On a Delta blues progression that Dylan had recorded
On the *Highway 61 Revisited* album, one of the grave mutterings
From *John Wesley Harding*, or a bittersweet lyrical song
From the 1975 *Blood on the Tracks* album, like "Buckets of Rain"
Or "You're Gonna Make Me Lonesome When You Go."

The Oxford County Blues

When summer folks brought their lawnmowers by on their way out to eat
At the Old Rowley Inn, for some funny reason known only to him,
Ancient Alton Rich rarely bothered to rise from his designated seat
To greet them out front of his workshop garage, more often than not
Waiting inside for those customers of his to come and find him sitting,
Not in the darkness exactly, and not necessarily alone,
But in a cone of gold light thrown by a head lamp, with his nephew,
    Donald Stone,
Who'd made a habit of checking on him ever since his wife had died.

Whatever his ostensible reason for staying put—aversion to the heat,
    allergies
To the tourist season—Alton obviously wasn't in much of a hurry
To hear how the fan belt seem to have snapped, how the blade
Had chipped on a rock, or how the choke, left open, had flooded
The motor with gasoline. He and Donald, a jovial man twice as young
As well as twice as large, kept to their respective chairs (matching black
Vinyl recliners) and with taciturn twinkles in their matching blue eyes
Looked up without even squinting without even blinking, without even
    showing
The slightest sign of surprise at the khaki-clad insurance man
Or the Scottish-plaid real-estate woman who'd walked through the door.

There they reclined, in jeans and flannel shirts, or drab green jumpsuits
Buttoned up the front, and no minor mechanical emergency
Could budge them from their chairs. In fact, it wouldn't be until the
    flatlander,
From one or another suburb of Boston, had altered not just the rhythm
Of his or her speech, but the inflection, tone, and pronunciation, too—
Dropping some r's and adding a drawl to suit the nasal occasion—
That Alton and Donald, sizing up the situation, would concede
To accompany their clients into the glare of the afternoon sun
And begin the inspection that would yield a diagnosis
And result in the promise that they'd have it fixed by the weekend.

Out in the driveway at the trunk of the Volvo, the hatch
Of the Honda, or the hitch of the Subaru Outback station wagon
That had a bike rack and a roof rack as well, kneeling to the mower
That Donald had helped him lower with a grunt to the ground,

Alton would say something inaudible that for no particular reason
Reminded Donald of tales that the summer people would tell
In the quaint colonial comfort of that inn up the hill, at a table
That would burn with the rest of the inn the winter after Alton had died.

While Alton knelt to fiddle with the choke, check the oil, or pull
The points and plugs for signs of a tired ignition, his nephew
Would entertain the summer folks with an up-country rendition
Of one or another story, going over it like a mower through grass.

There was the one about Donald getting so drunk on Kahlua
That he'd fallen on his butt one Saturday at the dance
At the fairgrounds pavilion, where one sign on the door reads, "BYOB—
Bring Your Own Bible," and another says, "It's six bucks cover, twelve
For a couple." The one about Alton gettin' pinched by the game warden
Up at Moosehead Lake fuh takin' too much trout"; and the one about "the fella
Who's had such a toyme of it since movin' up from Pahtland
That he dahn neah gets in a tussle with a black bayah
Whenever he takes the gahbage out." Yarns made of wool
That their ancestors had clipped from the backs of fat sheep
They'd raised on this land. Wool carded by hand—by women, by hearths—
In saltbox houses that no longer stand on the moose-trodden cart roads
On cellar-hole foundations up in the mountains, where you can still excavate
Your share of broken jugs and rusted steel tools.

From the moment those summer folks laid their squinting eyes on them
In the cave-like garage, both looking up with eyes as baby blue
As the bikini on the pin-up girl perched on the hood
Of the cherry-red convertible on the calendar behind them,
Above the greasy workbench—well, it was pretty much a given
That, at their dinners of new potatoes, arugula, and salmon (washed down
With white wine), Donald's stories would remind them
Of what else was blue in earthy green and gray Oxford County, Maine.

The blue beryl crystals mined from huge deposits of white quartz
In Bethel on Rattlesnake Mountain. The choppy blue surface
Of Lake Keewaydin up on Route 5 in poor old East Stoneham
When the clarifying northwest wind for which the lake was named
(From Longfellow's epic poem *Hiawatha*) blows down the odor

Of the paper mills on the Androscoggin. The blue vinyl house
Of the fire warden by the town hall in Albany where, more than once,
On his way to buy groceries at the IGA, Alton had seen a moose standing
In a field with a horse. And, also according to Donald, the blue ice
On the Crooked River, in early spring, behind Alton's trailer,
When the otters, "slidin' downstream on their bellies between them
    boulders,"
Entertained Alton at his breakfast of eggs and bacon and a weak cup of
    Folger's
On the trailer's back porch—"like they wuz tryin' out fuh the cihkus or
    sumthin'!"

Elegy for Omayra Sánchez

I could have stopped watching the reel about the mudslide
That buried the town of Armero in 1985
Any time I wanted. I didn't need to see, among
The many open windows on the screen of the laptop
Computer in my office, the seismological diagrams
That showed the results of the quaking and shaking
Of the snow-capped volcano, or the footage that followed
With multiple examples of the twenty thousand people
Who died when the earthquake shook loose the lava
And set into motion the wide rivers of sediment
That flooded the valley of *Nevado del Ruiz*
Before the authorities could plan a mass evacuation.
All I had to do, I knew, was click the little box
In the upper left-hand corner and go on to something else
Waiting on my computer. Even if it was related—
An exposé, for example, on the inability
Of the Colombian government during the 1980s
To do much of anything about the problems in the country—
It would have been more constructive than watching
Clips spliced from reports by television news crews
From a station in Bogotá that someone took the trouble
To post on YouTube, offering the world a close-up view.
I might have spent the time studying the weak attempt
Of one administration after another to keep
Its soldiers from killing *campesinos* in the mountains,
To pacify the FARC *guerrillas,* or to capture
Such *paramilitarios* responsible for the cocaine trade
As the merciless mercenaries of Pablo Escobar,
Who'd invaded the Palace of Justice just the week before
The burial of Armero, destroying the documents
That were about to be used to indict him
And abducting for execution more than twenty judges.
I'd already heard enough about the mudslide anyway
In the international news the week it happened
Thirty years before, and later on in a sad but good
Expository essay by a native of Colombia, busted
For smuggling coke at the airport in Boston,
Who wrote about it for me in my weekly class at prison.

That should have been enough to satisfy me for good.
I didn't need to sit there staring at the gruesome
Live footage they'd shown on voyeuristic television.

But the first scene, shot from a helicopter, was hard
To turn away from—roiling molten lava making
Billowing clouds of gray smoke and wisps of white steam
Swirl and spiral around the peak of the great volcano
When the melting of the six glaciers set in motion
The massive *lahars,* those "swift-moving currents
Of hot gas and rock" called "pyroclastic flows."
And then there were the camera's unblinking stares
At buildings in Armero up to their windows in mud,
Medics rushing the injured on stretchers to makeshift clinics
In emergency Red Cross tents, survivors trembling
In fear and sorrow to see what had happened,
And soldiers pulling bloated, mud-caked corpses
From inundated buildings once the waters subsided.
There were even interviews with several survivors
Who would go on living in the nearby valley towns
Of Guayabal and Lérida, in the state of Tolima,
In this region of Colombia known for its coffee,
Its tropical fruit, and its high-quality cotton,
In the south-central section of the three cordilleras
That run the length of the country, from Medellín south
To Cali, then all the way down to Chile from Perú.

I couldn't stop looking for the life of me after that—
Especially as I watched the story, at first in awe
And then in tears, of Omayra Sánchez, the teenaged girl,
Symbol forever after of the sorry disorganized state
Of Colombia back then, trapped in rising water,
Unable to budge her legs from the slab of cement
That had fallen on them, speaking to that camera
With an uncanny poise that I wanted to attribute
To the peace of mind Colombians find in simple company.
Over the course of three days, live on camera,
On the evening news in Bogotá, in the presence of strangers,
Rescue workers, priests, social workers, and engineers

Helpless to do much of anything for her, she waited
In vain to be freed, without even her mother, stranded
In Bogotá, or relatives drowned in the flood, there
To hold her—making do with a group of strangers.
All they could do, besides console her, was to help her
To tilt her head back so that she could receive,
Like the wine and wafer of the sacramental host,
Bits of *arepa* and sips of water, in a beatific twist
On a baptismal religious rite, to keep her alive
With food and encouraging talk, until, toward the end,
From her darkly encircled eyes, she looked directly into
The likewise encircled but unblinking eye of the camera
To say farewell to her family, missing in the mudslide
Or gone to Bogotá on business, and unable to return:

Si escuchas, Mami—If you are listening, Mother—
Te quiero. Les quiero a mi mamá y mi papá, I love you.
I love my mother and father. *A mis hermanos y tíos también.*
Que todo les vaya bien. And my siblings and aunts
And uncles as well. May all go well in life for you.
Y para esta gente que me ayude. And for these people
Who have helped me too, yes, for them as well
A final word, in choked-up fragments, of farewell.

ACKNOWLEDGMENTS

Able Muse: "The Orchard"
About Place: "The Trees of Heaven"
AGNI: "Screech Owl"; "First Impression"
The Chachalaca Review: "Jalapeño, Cacao, Pitarilla, Agave, Romero, y Tobaco"*
The Common Ground Review: "Plumbing"
Cutthroat: "Above the Fold"
Intima: A Journal of Narrative Medicine: "The Delivery"*
The Larcom Review: "The 47 Bus"
The Latin-American Literary Review: "Earth Day"; "Barrio Boston"
The Muddy River Poetry Review: "The Call"
The Naugatuck River Review: "Marshfield Party"**
Negative Capability: "My Eight-Year-Old Grandmother"
Nine Mile: "Injunction"; "Poplar Hollow Inventory"; "The Sonnet"
Ohio Today: "Athens County Breakdown"
Pangyrus: "At the Threshold"*; "Talisman"
Pleasure Boat Studios/"Lights" Zine: "At Hamilton and Pearl"; "Tenskwatawa"; "Tag"
Poems from the Wellspring: "The Assassination"*
Poetry Quarterly: "Memphis Bus Station" "Watercolor Portrait"**
Poetry Northwest: "On a Globe Hanging by Wire from a Classroom Ceiling"
Red Letters: "Traffic Jam"
The Short North Gazette: "The Bomb"
Sixfold: "At the Perryville Battlefield State Historic Site"; "One Autumn Day Last Year"; "At the Childhood Home of Ozzy Osbourne"; "Rain Dance"*; "Bicentennial"**
Solstice: "Queen for a Day"
The Somerville News: "In the Stately Greek Revival Architectural Style," "White Wooden Crosses"
Spitball: "Game Called Because of Rain"
The Tower Journal: "Elegy for Omayra Sánchez"
The Wild Leaf Anthology: "The Oxford County Blues"

*This poem—with four others similarly noted in the list of acknowledgments— is now incorporated in the longer poem "In the Southern-Most Mexican State of Chiapas."

**This poem—with two others similarly noted in the list of acknowledgments—is now incorporated in the longer poem "Soundtrack."

Scott Ruescher attended the Iowa Writers Workshop on a teaching-writing fellowship in the late 1970s and published his early poems widely—*in The Nation, Ploughshares, Poetry Northwest, Prairie Schooner, The Ohio Review,* and the like—but didn't find sustained inspiration and direction until he spent a month in residence at Vermont Studio Center in 1999. Two chapbooks, *Sidewalk Tectonics and Perfect Memory,* and one full-length collection—*Waiting for the Light to Change* (Prolific Press, 2017)—resulted from the momentum generated there.

Retired administrator of the Arts in Education program at Harvard Graduate School of Education, and former part-time English teacher for the Boston University Prison Education Program, he writes promotional copy for a community development corporation (The Neighborhood Developers) and works in ESOL and citizenship classrooms in the poor immigrant communities across the monstrous Tobin Bridge from glitzy downtown Boston.

www.ingramcontent.com/pod-product-compliance
Lightning Source LLC
Chambersburg PA
CBHW030054170426
43197CB00010B/1527